Strengthening Family Relationships

A four-week course to help adults discover a biblical foundation for loving and accepting their families.

by
Larry Keefauver

Apply·It·To·Life™
Adult
BIBLE CURRICULUM
from *Group*

Group®
Loveland, Colorado

Apply·It·To·Life™
Adult
BIBLE CURRICULUM

Group®

Strengthening Family Relationships
Copyright © 1995 Group Publishing, Inc.

All rights reserved. No part of this book may be reproduced in any manner whatsoever without prior written permission from the publisher, except where noted on handouts and in the case of brief quotations embodied in critical articles and reviews. For information, write Permissions, Group Publishing, Inc., Dept. BK, Box 481, Loveland, CO 80539.

Credits
Editors: Stephen Parolini and Bob Buller
Senior Editor: Paul Woods
Creative Products Director: Joani Schultz
Cover Designer: Liz Howe
Interior Designer: Kathy Benson
Cover Photographer: Natalie Pelafos; The Stock Market
Interior Illustrator: Amy Bryant

ISBN 1-55945-501-2

10 9 8 7 6 5 4 3 2 1   04 03 02 01 00 99 98 97 96 95

Printed in the United States of America.

CONTENTS

INTRODUCTION — 5

What Is Apply-It-To-Life™ Adult Bible Curriculum? — 5
What Makes Apply-It-To-Life Adult Bible Curriculum Unique? — 5
How to Use Apply-It-To-Life Adult Bible Curriculum — 10
Course Introduction: Strengthening Family Relationships — 14
Publicity Page — 16

LESSON 1 — 17

I Accept You
We can accept and respect family members.

LESSON 2 — 27

I Love You
We can demonstrate God's love to family members.

LESSON 3 — 37

I Forgive You
God wants us to forgive our family members as Christ has forgiven us.

LESSON 4 — 49

I Appreciate You
We can express sincere appreciation and thanks to family members.

FELLOWSHIP AND OUTREACH SPECIALS — 61

Introduction

WHAT IS APPLY-IT-TO-LIFE™ ADULT BIBLE CURRICULUM?

Apply-It-To-Life™ Adult Bible Curriculum is a series of four-week study courses designed to help you facilitate powerful lessons that will help class members grow in faith. Use this course with
- Sunday school classes,
- home study groups,
- weekday Bible study groups,
- men's Bible studies,
- women's Bible studies, and
- family classes.

The variety of courses gives the adult student a broad coverage of topical, life-related issues and significant biblical topics. In addition, as the name of the series implies, every lesson helps the adult student apply Scripture to his or her life.

Each course in Apply-It-To-Life Adult Bible Curriculum provides four lessons on different aspects of one topic. In each course, you also receive Fellowship and Outreach Specials connected to the month's topic. They provide suggestions for building closer relationships in your class, outreach activities, and even a party idea!

WHAT MAKES APPLY-IT-TO-LIFE ADULT BIBLE CURRICULUM UNIQUE?

Teaching as Jesus Taught

Jesus was a master teacher. With Apply-It-To-Life Adult Bible Curriculum, you'll use the same teaching methods and principles that Jesus used:

- **Active Learning.** Think back on an important lesson you've learned in life. Did you learn it from reading about it? from hearing about it? from something you did? Chances are, the most important lessons you've learned came from something you experienced. That's what active learning is—learning by doing. Active learning leads students through activities and experiences that help them understand important principles, messages, and ideas. It's a discovery process that helps people internalize and remember what they learn.

Jesus often used active learning. One of the most vivid examples is his washing of his disciples' feet. In Apply-It-To-Life Adult Bible Curriculum, the teacher might remove his or her shoes and socks then read aloud the foot-washing passage from John 13, or the teacher might choose to actually wash people's feet. Participants won't soon forget it. Active learning uses simple activities to teach profound lessons.

● **Interactive Learning.** Interactive learning means learning through small-group interaction and discussion. While it may seem to be a simple concept, it's radically new to many churches that have stuck with a lecture format or large-group discussion for so long. With interactive learning, each person is actively involved in discovering God's truth through talking with other people about God's Word. Interactive learning is discussion with a difference. It puts people in pairs, trios, or foursomes to involve everyone in the learning experience. It takes active learning a step further by having people who have gone through an experience teach others what they've learned.

Jesus often helped cement the learning from an experience by questioning people—sometimes in small groups—about what had happened. He regularly questioned his followers and his opponents, forcing them to think and to discuss among themselves what he was teaching them. After washing his disciples' feet, the first thing Jesus did was ask the disciples if they understood what he had done. After the "foot washing" activity, the teacher might form small groups and have people discuss how they felt when the leader removed his or her shoes and socks. Then group members could compare those feelings and the learning involved to what the disciples must have experienced.

● **Biblical Depth.** Apply-It-To-Life Adult Bible Curriculum recognizes that most adults are ready to go below the surface to better understand the deeper truths of the Bible. Therefore, the activities and studies go beyond an "easy answer" approach to Christian education and lead adults to grapple with difficult issues from a biblical perspective.

Each lesson begins by giving the teacher resource material on the Bible passages covered in the study. In the Bible Basis, you'll find information that will help you understand the Scriptures you're dealing with. Within the class-time section of the lesson, thought-provoking activities and discussions lead adults to new depths of biblical understanding. Bible Insights within the lesson give pertinent information that will bring the Bible to life for you and your class members. In-class handouts give adults significant Bible information and challenge them to search for and discover biblical truths for themselves. Finally, the "For Even Deeper Discussion" sections provide questions that will lead your class members to new and deeper levels of insight and application.

No one questions the depth of Jesus' teachings or the effectiveness of his teaching methods. This curriculum follows Jesus' example and helps people probe the depths of the Bible in a way no other adult curriculum does.

● **Bible Application.** Jesus didn't stop with helping people understand truth. For him, teaching took the learner beyond understanding to application. It wasn't enough that the rich young ruler knew all the right answers. Jesus wanted him to take action on what he knew. In the same way, Apply-It-To-Life Adult Bible Curriculum encourages a response in people's lives. That's why this curriculum is called "Apply-It-To-Life"! Depth of understanding means little if the truths of Scripture don't zing into people's hearts. Each lesson brings home one point and encourages people to consider the changes they might make in response.

● **One Purpose.** In each study, every activity works toward communicating and applying the same point. People may discover other new truths, but the study doesn't load them down with a mass of information. Sometimes less is more. When lessons try to teach too much, they often fail to teach anything. Even Jesus limited his teaching to what he felt people could really learn and apply (John 16:12). Apply-It-To-Life Adult Bible Curriculum makes sure that class members thoroughly understand and apply one point each week.

● **Variety.** People appreciate variety. Jesus constantly varied his teaching methods. One day he would have a serious discussion with his disciples about who he was and another day he'd baffle them by turning water into wine. What he didn't do was allow them to become bored with what he had to teach them.

Any kind of study can become less than exciting if the leader and students do everything the same way week after week. Apply-It-To-Life Adult Bible Curriculum varies activities and approaches to keep everyone's interest level high each week. In one class, you might have people in small groups "put themselves in the disciples' sandals" and experience something of the confusion of Jesus' death and resurrection. In another lesson, class members may experience problems in communication and examine how such problems can damage relationships.

To meet adults' varied needs, the courses cover a wide range of topics such as Jesus, knowing God's will, communication, taking faith to work, and highlights of Bible books. One month you may choose to study a family or personal faith issue; the next month you may cover a biblical topic such as the book of John.

● **Relevance.** People today want to know how to live successfully right now. They struggle with living as authentic Christians at work, in the family, and in the community. Most churchgoing adults want to learn about the Bible, but not merely for the sake of having greater Bible knowledge. They want to know how the Bible can help them live faithful lives—how it can help them face the difficulties of living in today's culture. Apply-It-To-Life Adult Bible Curriculum bridges the gap between biblical truth and the "real world" issues of people's lives. Jesus didn't discuss with his followers the eschatological significance of Ezekiel's wheels, and Apply-It-To-Life Adult Bible Curriculum won't either! Courses and studies in this curriculum focus on the real needs of people and help them discover answers in Scripture that will help meet those needs.

● **A Nonthreatening Atmosphere.** In many adult classes, people feel intimidated because they're new Christians or because they don't have the Bible knowledge they think they should have. Jesus sometimes intimidated those who opposed him, but he consistently treated his followers with understanding and respect. We want people in church to experience the same understanding and respect Jesus' followers experienced. With Apply-It-To-Life Adult Bible Curriculum, no one is embarrassed for not knowing or understanding as much as someone else. In fact, the interactive learning process minimizes the differences between those with vast Bible knowledge and those with little Bible knowledge. Lessons often begin with nonthreatening, sharing questions and move slowly toward more depth. Whatever their level of knowledge or commitment, class members will work together to discover biblical truths that can affect their lives.

● **A Group That Cares.** Jesus began his ministry by choosing a group of 12 people who learned from him together. That group practically lived together—sharing one another's hurts, joys, and ambitions. Sometimes Jesus divided the 12 into smaller groups and worked with just three or four at a time.

Studies have shown that many adults today long for a close-knit group of people with whom they can share personal needs and joys. And people interact more freely when they feel accepted in a group. Activities in this curriculum will help class members get to know one another better and care for one another more as they study the Bible and apply its truths to their lives. As people reveal their thoughts and feelings to one another, they'll grow closer and develop more commitment to the group and to each other. And they'll be encouraging one another along the way!

• **An Element of Delight.** We don't often think about Jesus' ministry in this way, but there certainly were times he brought fun and delight to his followers. Remember the time he raised Peter's mother-in-law? or the time he sat happily with children on his lap? How about the joy and excitement at his triumphal entry into Jerusalem? or the time he helped fishing disciples catch a boatload of fish—after they'd fished all night with no success?

People learn more when they're having fun. So within Apply-It-To-Life Adult Bible Curriculum, elements of fun and delight pop up often. And sometimes adding fun is as simple as using a carrot for a pretend microphone!

Taking the Fear out of Teaching

Teachers love Apply-It-To-Life Adult Bible Curriculum because it makes teaching much less stressful. Lessons in this curriculum

• **are easy to teach.** Interactive learning frees the teacher from being a dispenser of information to serve as a facilitator of learning. Teachers can spend class time guiding people to discover and apply biblical truths. The studies provide clear, understandable Bible background; easy-to-prepare learning experiences; and powerful, thought-provoking discussion questions.

• **can be prepared quickly.** Lessons in Apply-It-To-Life Adult Bible Curriculum are logical and clear. There's no sorting through tons of information to figure out the lesson. In 30 minutes, a busy teacher can easily read a lesson and prepare to teach it. In addition, optional and For Extra Time activities allow the teacher to tailor the lesson to the class. And the thorough instructions and questions will guide even an inexperienced teacher through each powerful lesson.

• **let everyone share in the class's success.** With Apply-It-To-Life Adult Bible Curriculum, the teacher is one of the participants. The teacher still guides the class, but the burden is not as heavy. Everyone participates and adds to the study's effectiveness. So when the study has an impact, everyone shares in that success.

• **lead the teacher to new discoveries.** Each lesson is designed to help the teacher first discover a biblical truth. And most teachers will make additional discoveries as they prepare each lesson. In class, the teacher will discover even more as other adults share what they have found. As with any type of teaching, the teacher will likely learn more than anyone else in the class!

● **provide relevant information to class members.** Photocopiable handouts are designed to help people better understand or interpret Bible passages. And the handouts make teaching easier because the teacher can often refer to them for small-group discussion questions and instructions.

How to Use Apply-It-To-Life Adult Bible Curriculum

First familiarize yourself with an Apply-It-To-Life Adult Bible Curriculum lesson. The following explanations will help you understand how the lesson elements work together.

Lesson Elements

● The **Opening** maps out the lesson's agenda and introduces your class to the topic for the session. Sometimes this activity will help people get better acquainted as they begin to explore the topic together.

● The **Bible Exploration and Application** activities will help people discover what the Bible says about the topic and how the lesson's point applies to their lives. In these varied activities, class members find answers to the "So what?" question. Through active and interactive learning methods, people will discover the relevance of the Scriptures and commit to growing closer to God.

You may use either one or both of the options in this section. They are designed to stand alone or to work together. Both present the same point in different ways. "For Even Deeper Discussion" questions appear at the end of each activity in this section. Use these questions whenever you feel they might be particularly helpful for your class.

● The **Closing** pulls everything in the lesson together and often funnels the lesson's message into a time of reflection and prayer.

● The **For Extra Time** section is just that. Use it when you've completed the lesson and still have time left or when you've used one Bible Exploration and Application option and don't have time to do the other. Or you might plan to use it instead of another option.

When you put all the sections together, you get a lesson that's fun and easy to teach. Plus, participants will learn truths they'll remember and apply to their daily lives.

About the Questions and Answers

The answers given after discussion questions are responses participants *might* give. They aren't the only answers or the "right" answers. However, you can use them to spark discussion.

Real life doesn't always allow us to give the "right" answers. That's why some of the responses given are negative or controversial. If someone responds negatively, don't be shocked. Accept the person and use the opportunity to explore other perspectives on the issue.

To get more out of your discussions, use follow-up inquiries such as
- Tell me more.
- What do you mean by that?
- What makes you feel that way?

Guidelines for a Successful Adult Class

- **Be a facilitator, not a lecturer.** Apply-It-To-Life Adult Bible Curriculum is student-based rather than teacher-based. Your job is to direct the activities and facilitate the discussions. You become a choreographer of sorts: someone who gets everyone else involved in the discussion and keeps the discussion on track.
- **Teach adults how to form small groups.** Help adults discover the benefits of small-group discussions by assisting them in forming groups of four, three, or two—whatever the activity calls for. Small-group sharing allows for more discussion and involvement by all participants. It's not as threatening or scary to open up to two people as it would be to 20 or 200!

Some leaders decide not to form small groups because they want to hear everybody's ideas. The intention is good, but some people just won't talk in a large group. Use a "report back" time after small-group discussions to gather the best responses from all groups.

When you form small groups, don't always let people choose those right around them. Try creative group-forming methods to help everyone in the class get to know one another. For example, tell class members: find three other people wearing the same color you are; join two other people who like the same music you do; locate three others who shop at the same grocery store you do; find one who was born the same month as you; choose three who like the same season as you, and so on. If you have fun with it, your class will, too!

- **Encourage relationship building.** George Barna, in his insightful book about the church, *The Frog in the Kettle,* explains that adults today have a strong need to develop friendships. In a society of high-tech toys, "personal" computers, and lonely commutes, people long for positive human contact. That's where our church classes and groups can jump in. Help adults form friendships through your class. What's discovered in a classroom setting will be better applied when friends support each other outside the classroom. In fact, the relationships begun in your class may be as important as the truths you help your adults learn.

- **Be flexible.** Sometimes your class will complete every activity in the lesson with great success and wonderful learning. But what should you do if people go off on a tangent? or they get stuck in one of the activities? What if you don't have time to finish the lesson?

Don't panic. People learn best when they are interested and engaged in meaningful discussion, when they move at their own pace. And if you get through even one activity, your class will discover the point for the whole lesson. So relax. It's OK if you don't get everything done. Try to get to the Closing in every lesson, since its purpose is to bring closure to the topic for the week. But if you don't, don't sweat it!

- **Expect the unexpected.** Active learning is an adventure that doesn't always take you where you think you're going. Don't be surprised if things don't go exactly the way you'd planned. Be open to the different directions the Holy Spirit may lead your class. When something goes wrong or an unexpected emotion is aroused, take advantage of this teachable moment. Ask probing questions, follow up on someone's deep need or concern. Those moments are often the best opportunities for learning that come our way.

- **Participate—and encourage participation.** Apply-It-To-Life Adult Bible Curriculum is only as interactive as you and your class make it. Learning arises out of dialogue. People need to grapple with and verbalize their questions and discoveries. Jump into discussions yourself, but don't "take over." Encourage everyone to participate. You can facilitate smooth discussions by using "active listening" responses such as rephrasing and summing up what's been said. If people seem stumped, use the possible responses after each question to spark further discussion. You may feel like a cheerleader at times, but your efforts will be worth it. The more people participate, the more they'll discover God's truths for themselves.

• **Trust the Holy Spirit.** All the previous six guidelines and the instructions in the lessons will be irrelevant if you ignore the presence of God in your classroom. God sent the Holy Spirit as our helper. As you use this curriculum, ask the Holy Spirit to help you facilitate the lessons. And ask the Holy Spirit to direct your class toward God's truth. Trust that God's Spirit can work through each person's discoveries, not just the teacher's.

How to Use This Course

Before the Four-Week Session
• Read the Course Introduction and This Course at a Glance (pp. 14-15).
• Decide how you'll use the art on the Publicity Page (p. 16) to publicize the course. Prepare fliers, newsletter articles, and posters as needed.
• Look at the Fellowship and Outreach Specials (p. 61) and decide which ones you'll use.

Before Each Lesson
• Read the one-sentence Point, the Objectives, and the Bible Basis for the lesson. The Bible Basis provides background information on the lesson's passages and shows how those passages relate to people today.
• Choose which activities you'll use from the lesson. Remember, it's not important to do every activity. Pick the ones that best fit your group and time allotment.
• Gather necessary supplies. They're listed in This Lesson at a Glance.
• Read each section of the lesson. Adjust activities as necessary to fit your class size and meeting room, but be careful not to delete all the activity. People learn best when they're actively involved in the learning process.

Course Introduction: Strengthening Family Relationships

What distinguishes a Christian's perspective of family from any other view of family in our society? And what does that perspective imply about a Christian's actions, thoughts, and values in the midst of "experiencing" family?

As Christians in relationships with family members (both Christian and non-Christian), we face unique challenges in living out what it means to be Christ-centered. In addition, we face dynamic questions we must constantly strive to answer with our lives—questions such as

- How can we accept family members as unique individuals and new creations in Christ?
- What is genuine love in the family?
- How can we forgive family members when they hurt us physically, mentally, or emotionally?
- How can we express sincere appreciation to one another without condoning sinful actions or attitudes?

In the Bible we discover that God chose the family to be the crucible in which we learn about and experience God's Word, love, forgiveness, acceptance, and affirmation. In the beginning, God created the family (Genesis 1–4). God chose Abram and his family to be a blessing for all the nations (Genesis 12–13). And God sent his only Son, Jesus, into a family to be raised, loved, and nurtured (Matthew 1–2; Luke 1–2). Finally, the family is a place to model God's love to the church and to the world (Ephesians 5–6). Now that's a challenge.

This four-week course will help adults understand God's instructions and incorporate them into daily family relationships. People will discover biblical insights for strengthening these relationships, and they'll learn to love their families in new and powerful ways.

With God's help, your class members will begin to implement life-changing attitudes and behaviors built on God's Word that will help them grow in their family relationships.

This Course at a Glance

Before you dive into the lessons, familiarize yourself with each lesson's point. Then read the Scripture passages.

- Study them as a background to the lessons.
- Use them as a basis for your personal devotions.
- Think about how they relate to people's situations today.

Lesson 1: I Accept You
The Point: We can accept and respect family members.
Bible Basis: Romans 14:1-18; 15:7; and Ephesians 5:21–6:4

Lesson 2: I Love You
The Point: We can demonstrate God's love to family members.
Bible Basis: 1 Corinthians 13:4-8; 1 John 3:11-24; and 1 John 4:7-21

Lesson 3: I Forgive You
The Point: God wants us to forgive our family members as Christ has forgiven us.
Bible Basis: Matthew 18:21-35; Colossians 3:12-14; and Matthew 6:12-15

Lesson 4: I Appreciate You
The Point: We can express sincere appreciation and thanks to family members.
Bible Basis: Psalm 145:1-7; 139:13-14; and Acts 15:22-33

PUBLICITY PAGE

Grab your congregation's attention! Add the vital details to the ready-made flier below, photocopy it, and use it to advertise this course on strengthening the family. Insert the flier in your bulletins. Enlarge it to make posters. Splash the art or anything else from this page in newsletters, bulletins, or even on postcards! It's that simple.

*The art from this page is also available on Group's MinistryNet™ computer on-line resource for you to manipulate on your computer. Call **800-447-1070** for information.*

Strengthening Family Relationships

A four-week adult course on loving and accepting family.

COME TO

ON

AT

COME LEARN MORE ABOUT HOW YOU CAN IMPROVE YOUR FAMILY RELATIONSHIPS—NO MATTER HOW GOOD OR BAD THEY ARE NOW!

Apply-It-To-Life™ Adult BIBLE CURRICULUM from Group

Strengthening Family Relationships

Strengthening Family Relationships

Permission to photocopy this page granted for local church use. Copyright © Group Publishing, Inc., Box 481, Loveland, CO 80539.

Lesson 1

I Accept You

We can accept and respect family members.

◀ THE POINT

OBJECTIVES

Participants will
- discover biblical teachings about acceptance,
- learn the difference between accepting people and condoning sinful or destructive behaviors, and
- identify practical ways to express their acceptance and respect for family members.

BIBLE BASIS

Look up the Scriptures. Then read the background paragraphs to see how the passages relate to people today.

In **Romans 14:1-18 and 15:7,** Paul instructs Christians to accept one another as Christ has accepted them.

Paul knew that some in the Roman church weren't accepting others. The issue separating people apparently was related to the observance of Jewish traditions (see Bible Insight, p. 21). However, Paul points out that it is part of a bigger issue: accepting others who are at a different level of maturity. Christians don't have any right to reject someone God has accepted.

Paul recognized that in any group of Christians—in the family or in the church—some will have weaker faith than others. We're instructed not to judge one another but to accept one another and to be sensitive to the beliefs and needs of those who don't think exactly as we do.

In accepting others, we're expected to live up to a high standard: We're to accept others as Christ accepts us. That probably relates in some degree back to Paul's explanation of Christ's actions in Romans 5: "While we were still sinners, Christ died for us." Jesus accepted us and died for us before we ever turned to him. That's a terrific example of a selfless acceptance of others.

ROMANS 14:1-18;
15:7

Paul also points out that accepting others isn't just for the purpose of building relationships. In the end, as we accept someone and lead that person to a more mature relationship with Jesus, we will bring praise to God.

EPHESIANS 5:21–6:4

Ephesians 5:21–6:4 takes the quality of acceptance even further. According to this passage, we're to submit to and serve one another out of respect for Jesus. Wives are specifically told to submit to husbands, but it's interesting to note that "submit" doesn't equal "obey." Obedience is sometimes a forced submission, and that's not what Paul is suggesting. In fact, nowhere in Scripture are wives told to obey husbands. Submission here means a voluntary giving up of one's own rights out of love for Christ. And husbands are told to love their wives with the same attitude of servanthood that Christ demonstrated in giving his life for us. That sounds even stronger than "submit." Husbands are commanded to give up their own rights and wishes for the good of their wives.

In a parent-child relationship, parents demonstrate respect by *not* exasperating their children or provoking them to anger. Fathers aren't to be arbitrary and vindictive but are to teach and model Jesus for their children. And children, according to Paul (echoing Exodus 20:12), are to obey their parents and hold them in high regard, even if children don't agree with everything their parents say and do.

Thus, according to Paul, a loving, serving attitude is the key in every relationship described in this passage. Paul doesn't tell anyone to be harsh and demanding, but instead he instructs us to show understanding, love, and acceptance to all in our families.

To accept means to honor, respect, and love one another. Accepting people doesn't mean condoning sin in their lives, but it does mean loving them in spite of their sin—as Jesus does. This lesson helps people explore ways they can accept all family members, even those who have done things to damage family relationships.

This Lesson at a Glance

Section	Minutes	What Participants Will Do	Supplies
Opening	up to 10	**Family Sayings**—Learn what today's lesson is about and tell each other about wise family sayings from their childhood.	
Bible Exploration and Application	15 to 25	☐ Option 1: **Accepting the Acceptable**—Determine what Romans 14:1-18 and 15:7 say about accepting others.	Bibles, newsprint, markers
	20 to 30	☐ Option 2: **God's Acceptance**—Examine Romans 15:7 and Ephesians 5:21—6:4 and determine what accepting family members really means.	Bibles, "Accepted by Christ" handouts (p. 25), pencils
Closing	up to 10	**Accept, Serve, and Honor**—Write messages expressing acceptance and love.	Paper, pencils or pens
For Extra Time	up to 10	**Tough to Accept**—List reasons to accept family members who aren't easy to accept.	Paper, pencils
	up to 10	**Prayer Time**—Share concerns about family relationships and pray together.	

OPENING

Family Sayings
(up to 10 minutes)

As you begin the class, tell class members what you'll be learning in today's lesson. Use the following statement or your own summary of the main point: **Welcome to the first week of four in our study on strengthening family relationships. In this study, we're going to focus on what it means to live out Christ-centered attitudes and behaviors in our families.**

Open with prayer. Then encourage class members to get involved in the discussions and activities during the study.

Have everyone stand, mingle, and for the next three minutes tell at least five other people about one or more family sayings they remember from childhood. Family sayings are clichés or "wise words" they might have heard repeatedly while growing up (for example, "If it ain't broke, don't fix it" or "Wait until your father gets home"). People can tell the same sayings to each person they talk to. Then have adults sit down with partners and share insights from their discussions.

Have partners discuss the following:

● **What sayings were most unique? most common? most biblically based?** Answers will vary.

● **How did you feel when you heard those family sayings as a child? when you recalled them just now?** (I was hurt by what my dad said; we didn't listen to them after a while.)

Say: **It can be fun or painful to recall sayings our parents and siblings used when we were children. While some sayings were fun or silly, others were hurtful and full of anger. For some of us, family experiences have not been very positive. But God wants us to ▶ accept and respect our family members. Let's explore what that means.**

TEACHER TIP

Your class members probably come from many different family situations. Some may have lived through abuse when they were younger. Some may still experience abuse. Still others may be frustrated by daily arguments with their children.

While family situations differ, the principles and truths in this course are applicable to all family members. Ask participants to apply their discoveries to their own family situations. Encourage people to tell about their specific situations. The whole class will benefit.

THE POINT ▶

BIBLE EXPLORATION AND APPLICATION

☐ OPTION 1:
Accepting the Acceptable
(15 to 25 minutes)

Form groups of no more than four. Have groups look up and read Romans 14:1-18; 15:7 and discuss the following questions. Have groups report insights to the whole class after each question. Ask:

● **Why are we to accept others?**

- What are we to avoid in our relationships with others?
- What do these verses tell us about God's desire for us ▷ to accept and respect family members?

After a couple of minutes of discussion, go around the room and randomly take people out of their groups and place them in others. Do this at least once to each group without explaining why you're rearranging the groups.

After about seven minutes, get adults' attention and ask the following questions:

- **According to the Bible, who are we to accept?** (Weaker people; people who have different beliefs; brothers and sisters in Christ.)
- **What did you discover in this passage about the importance of accepting and respecting others?** (We accept others because God accepts us; we're to accept others because they're God's servants, too.)
- **What was it like to be removed from one group and placed in another?** (Confusing; difficult; unsettling.)
- **How is the way you did or didn't accept the new person into your group like or unlike the way you accept family members?** (It's similar—we didn't reach out much in our group, and that's how I act with relatives; it's different because we accepted our new group member right away.)
- **What keeps us from fully accepting family members?** (Things they've done to us in the past; attitudes; lack of love for us.)

Say: **In Paul's day, Christians often judged one another based on dietary practices or the observance of certain holy days. Their acceptance of fellow Christians was often based on the conclusions of their judgment. What things do we judge family members for today?**

People may suggest things like bad attitudes, smoking, or rudeness. List on newsprint the ideas people call out. Then have people quickly turn to partners to discuss the following questions in light of the newsprint list:

- **How do these items affect the way we accept family members?**
- **What is the difference between accepting others and accepting their behaviors or lifestyles? How can we apply the message of Romans to our relationships with family members?**

Have volunteers share their insights with the rest of the class. Then say: **Accepting our family members doesn't mean we have to condone their behaviors or lifestyles. Let's see what Ephesians says about accepting family members.**

◁ THE POINT

BIBLE INSIGHT

Paul's reference in this passage to people "whose faith is weak" probably described Jewish Christians who still clung to some of the traditions of Judaism such as observing the Sabbath, not eating certain foods, and celebrating certain holy days. Paul says we should not reject people like this who have faith in Jesus and sincerely believe they are doing what God wants them to. A life of righteousness, peace, and joy in the Holy Spirit shows a person's true faith (Romans 14:17-18).

▪▪▪▪▪▪▪▪▪▪▪▪▪▪▪▪▪▪▪▪▪▪▪▪▪▪▪▪

FOR *Even Deeper* DISCUSSION

Form groups of no more than four and discuss the following questions:

• What would it take for you to accept someone who had seriously abused you in some way? Is that kind of acceptance possible? Is it required by Christ?

• How much does your acceptance of a person reflect an acceptance of that person's actions? Explain.

• Could a person ever do something for which we should refuse to accept that person? Explain.

▪▪▪▪▪▪▪▪▪▪▪▪▪▪▪▪▪▪▪▪▪▪▪▪▪▪▪▪

☐ **OPTION 2:**
God's Acceptance
(20 to 30 minutes)

Before class, make one photocopy of the "Accepted by Christ" handout (p. 25) for each person.

Form all-new groups of no more than three people. Have people share in their groups messages of acceptance they'd like to hear from family members. After about three minutes, get everyone's attention and read aloud Romans 15:7. Say: **If we want to receive those messages of acceptance, we will probably need to give to our family members the same kinds of acceptance. God wants us to accept one another as Jesus accepts us. Let's take a look at our model for accepting others.**

Distribute handouts and pencils. Have class members remain in their groups as they individually complete section 1 of the "Accepted by Christ" handout. Then have people discuss in their groups the questions in section 2 of the handout.

After about five minutes, gather adults together and have them report on their discussions. Then ask:

• **How is the way Jesus accepts us an example for the way we should accept others?**

• **What kinds of things did Jesus choose to overlook in accepting us?**

• **What kinds of things do we sometimes need to overlook in accepting family members?**

Say: **In your group, read silently Ephesians 5:21–6:4 and search the passages together for action words (verbs) that might refer to acceptance (such as "submit," "love," and "present" themselves). List these on the back of your handout.**

After about two minutes, have volunteers call out the words they discovered. Assign each group one of those

BIBLE INSIGHT

The Greek word translated "accept" in the New International Version of Romans 15:7 means "to grant one access to one's heart, to take into friendship." Thus, it describes emotional as well as intellectual acceptance. We must love family members no matter how different they are from our expectations. To accept as Jesus did means to love others even when they don't love you.

Condoning sinful behavior is another matter. As hard as it sometimes seems, we can love others—as God does—even when their behavior is unacceptable. However, that doesn't mean that we just ignore what a person does or that we constantly badger family members about their behavior. Love means doing what's best for other people. Sometimes that involves silent disapproval, and sometimes it means loving confrontation of wrongdoing in people's lives.

Accepted by Christ

Section 1

Read the definition of acceptance.

> ### Acceptance
> The Greek word for "accept" means "to take to one's self; to receive; to befriend; or to lead along side of." Acceptance means to be a friend, to form a relationship that can guide and help another person. Instead of judging family members, we're to accept and encourage them in their walk with Christ.

Now read the following passages, keeping in mind the definition of acceptance. In the space under each passage, list ways the passage relates to Christ's acceptance of those who believe in him and ways it relates to your family relationships.

1. A child of God—John 1:12 *belief – right*

2. No longer servants, but friends—John 15:15

    gives us the truth –

3. God's Spirit lives in you—1 Corinthians 3:16

    Reside

4. No longer foreigners, but fellow citizens—Ephesians 2:19-20

5. Living stones—1 Peter 2:5

6. Included in Christ when you believe—Ephesians 1:13-14

Section 2

- What does it mean to be accepted by Christ?
- Of the Scriptural descriptions of Christ's acceptance, which is most meaningful to you? Why?
- How can you live out the Bible's descriptions in your relationships with family members?

LESSON 1

I Accept You

APPLY-IT-TO LIFE THIS WEEK

The Point: ▶ We can accept and respect family members.
Scripture Focus: Romans 14:1-18; 15:7; and Ephesians 5:21–6:4

Reflecting on God's Word

Each day this week, read one of the following Scripture passages and examine how the Bible characters demonstrated (or failed to demonstrate) acceptance or respect. List your discoveries in the spaces under the passages.

Day 1: Genesis 33. Esau and Jacob.

Day 2: Ruth 3. Boaz and Ruth.

Day 3: 1 Samuel 24. Saul and David.

Day 4: Esther 5. Esther and the king.

Day 5: Luke 19. Jesus and Zacchaeus.

Day 6: Acts 9. Barnabas and Saul.

Beyond Reflection

1. Some Bible scholars suggest that what's difficult for us to accept in others can produce "pearls" in our lives just as the irritations from the sand produce pearls in oysters. Think of times in your life when irritations from another family member caused you to grow spiritually. Then talk with a family member about your discoveries and thank God together that difficult situations can bring growth.

2. Go to your local library and skim a book or two about what causes racism and prejudice. Then compare the reasons people are prejudiced toward others with the reasons people have a difficult time accepting or respecting family members. How is the lack of respect or acceptance of family members like or unlike prejudice?

Next Week's Bible Passages: 1 Corinthians 13:4-8; 1 John 3:11-24; and 1 John 4:7-21

Permission to photocopy this handout from Group's Apply-It-To-Life™ Adult Bible Curriculum granted for local church use.
Copyright © Group Publishing, Inc., Box 481, Loveland, CO 80539.

Lesson 2
I Love You

We can demonstrate God's love to family members.   ◀ THE POINT

OBJECTIVES

Participants will
- explore biblical teachings on God's love,
- evaluate the way they love family members,
- experience showing love through actions, and
- uncover practical ways to show God's love in their families.

BIBLE BASIS

Look up the Scriptures. Then read the background paragraphs to see how the passages relate to adults today.

In **1 Corinthians 13:4-8,** Paul defines God's love.   **1 CORINTHIANS 13:4-8**

We often associate this chapter with romantic love or love between husband and wife. Certainly the principles in the passage apply to that kind of love, but Paul gave this exposition on love within the context of instructions for the church concerning spiritual gifts. The main application of these principles should be to relationships among Christians.

Paul's definition of love comes from the way he sees God's love and gives us a clear picture of the selfless and giving nature of true love. To define this powerful kind of love, Paul describes what love is and what it isn't.

Love isn't selfish. A person who really loves someone wants the best for that person, even if it may not be what the person doing the loving wants. A loving person is not demanding, does not respond in anger or rudeness when provoked, never keeps a tally of what's owed, and is never glad when things go wrong for a friend or an enemy. On this point, Paul's language reminds us of the Golden Rule and Jesus' command to love not only those who love us but even our enemies (Luke 6:27-35).

Love is giving. A loving person always thinks the best of another, giving the benefit of any doubt. And he or she is always glad—never jealous—when things go well for another. The loving person is patient, never giving up on another, no matter how much rejection he or she experiences; there's always hope.

In the family, patience is often the most difficult aspect of love to express. And what family hasn't dealt with anger spinning out of control? Overcoming these negative tendencies is the greatest challenge in showing true love in the family. By meeting this challenge head-on, Christians can experience glimpses of God's own love in their family relationships.

1 JOHN 3:11-24

In **1 John 3:11-24,** the writer explains that we should love one another.

John uses the Old Testament story of Cain and Abel as an example of what not to do (hate others) in your own family. After mentioning the story of Cain and Abel, he concludes that anyone who doesn't love can't belong to God. Being in Christ means that we must obey God's command to love one another.

John then gives an example of true love: caring so much for someone that you're willing to give up your life for that person—as Jesus did for us. John says we should have that kind of selfless love for our fellow Christians. That's tough! He elaborates on that kind of love: He says that if we really have God's love in us and we really love others, we'll be unable to ignore people in need. We'll feel compelled to do what we can to remedy their need. To John, loving someone means real action on behalf of other people. He even suggests that if we don't act to help others, we haven't really experienced God's love ourselves.

1 JOHN 4:7-21

Then, in **1 John 4:7-21,** John reminds us that the source of true love is God. When we love one another, God lives in us and his love flows through us. And God's love drives out the fear in relationships. Fear and hate have no place in the Christian's definition of family. People who use fear or anger to control or manipulate their families disobey God. Instead, Christians must embrace God's love and express that love to family members—even when the lack of reciprocal love makes that difficult.

What is biblical love in the family? The Greek word for love in this passage (agape) is an unselfish, caring love that seeks the best for others without thought of return or personal reward. That's the kind of love John talks about in 1 John 3:16-18. But sometimes it's difficult to express that kind of love in the family. True love for our family members dictates that we be truthful and yet kind, firm and yet giving in our relationships.

This Lesson at a Glance

Section	Minutes	What Participants Will Do	Supplies
Opening	up to 5	**Love and the Family**—Learn what today's lesson is about.	Chalkboard and chalk or newsprint and markers
Bible Exploration and Application	25 to 35	☐ *Option 1:* **Expressing God's Love**—Explore and experience God's love in 1 Corinthians 13:4-8.	Bibles, "God's Love" handouts (p. 35), pencils
	15 to 25	☐ *Option 2:* **Love Without Fear and Hate**—Read 1 John 3:11-24 and 4:7-21, and brainstorm practical ways to overcome fear and hate in their families.	Bibles, newsprint, tape, markers
Closing	up to 10	**Saying "I Love You"**—Uncover practical ways to express God's love in their families.	Pencils
For Extra Time	up to 10	**The Toughest Person to Love**—Talk and pray about family members who are difficult to love.	
	up to 10	**Love Checklist**—Develop a checklist to remind them to express God's love daily.	Paper, pencils

OPENING

Love and the Family
(up to 5 minutes)

THE POINT ▷

Before class, draw a big heart on a chalkboard or newsprint and display it in front of the class.

As you begin the class, remind the group of last week's main point: **We can accept and respect family members.** Invite people to share insights from the past week relating to the point. Spend a few minutes exploring with people how easy or difficult it was to accept and respect family members throughout the week.

Then tell people what you'll be focusing on in today's lesson. Whet their appetites by telling them some of the things you'll be doing. Use the following statement or your own summary of the main point: **Welcome to our second study on affirming the family. In this study, we're going to have some fun learning ▷ how to better express God's love in our families.**

Open with prayer. Then encourage class members to get involved in the discussions and activities during the study.

BIBLE EXPLORATION AND APPLICATION

☐ OPTION 1: Expressing God's Love
(25 to 35 minutes)

Before class, make one photocopy of the "God's Love" handout (p. 35) for each person.

Form groups of no more than four. Have people form small circles with their chairs if possible (or turn to face each other).

Say: **Beginning with the person who comes from the largest immediate family, take turns telling one or more ways you've seen love expressed in your family. You might choose to tell about your spouse and children or about situations from your childhood. For example, you might tell about family members writing positive notes to one another. Or you might describe how members of your family kept you focused on your goals when you were a teenager.**

After four or five minutes, call time and have volunteers tell the rest of the class about the expressions of love they learned about from group members.

Then say: **We express love in many different ways. Now we're going to take a look at some ways the**

TEACHER TIP

For people who come from negative family situations, this may be a difficult exercise. Encourage adults to describe ways they show love in their families if they can't think of ways others have shown love to them.

Bible suggests we express love to one another.

Distribute a copy of the "God's Love" handout and a pencil to each person. Have people choose partners and read aloud 1 Corinthians 13:4-8 then complete the handouts independently. After a few minutes, have partners share their observations and discuss the questions on the handout.

Then have partners choose one aspect of God's love (from the handout) and brainstorm a way to express that love to at least two other people in the class. For example, if a pair chose "serving," they might offer to get coffee for other class members. A pair that chose "hopeful" might ask others about their dreams and express sincere hope that those people might realize their dreams.

Encourage creativity in the ways pairs express aspects of God's love. Allow about 10 minutes for pairs to express their love to one another. Then form groups of four by pairing up pairs. Have pairs number off from one to four and take turns answering the following questions (choose which "number" will go first to answer each question). Allow about two minutes for each question. Ask:

● **What was it like to express love to people you may not have known very well?** (Uncomfortable; fun; interesting.)

● **How is this different from the experience of expressing love to family members?** (Sometimes it's easier to show love to people you don't know; showing love to family members is more sincere.)

● **Which aspects of God's love were easiest to express during this activity? Explain.** (Serving, because we could do it in a limited amount of time; hopefulness, because it's not difficult to hope for people; kindness, because it's easy to show kindness.)

● **What does this experience tell us about expressing those aspects of love in our families?** (We can easily show kindness to family members; some aspects of love are very visual or experiential.)

● **Which aspects of God's love were most difficult to express during this activity? Explain.** (Patience, because patience requires a reason for being patient; humility, because humility is quiet and isn't expressed through actions.)

● **What does this experience tell us about expressing those aspects of love in our families?** (Some aspects of love take time; some aspects of God's love are invisible or unseen.)

Say: **We express our love to family members in different ways. While some people may be more demonstrative in their love, others are quiet and shy**

BIBLE INSIGHT

The word translated "love" in this passage is the Greek *agape*. This Greek word was not used much prior to the New Testament. In fact, it appears that Christians picked up this word and used it to refer to the kind of love shown to us by Christ in his death on the cross. This kind of love gives all and demands nothing. It is love for the unworthy—love described in Romans 5:8, where Paul talks about God loving us so much that he sent Jesus to die for us even though we were still sinners. In humans, this kind of love springs from the indwelling Holy Spirit and not from natural human affection.

THE POINT ▷

expressing their feelings. It's not always easy to express love, because fear or anger can get in the way. ▷ But we can demonstrate God's love to family members by keeping in mind the principles of love in 1 Corinthians 13.

■■■■■■■■■■■■■■■■■■■■■■■■■■■

FOR *Even Deeper* DISCUSSION

Form groups of no more than four and discuss the following questions:

● Could a family member ever do anything so bad or so many times that we would be justified in withdrawing our love? Explain.

● When might real love for a family member make us do something that person might see as hateful? When might an action perceived as loving turn out to be damaging?

● Paul says, "Love never fails." Is that true? Does it always seem to be true? Explain.

■■■■■■■■■■■■■■■■■■■■■■■■■■■

☐ **OPTION 2:**
Love Without Fear and Hate
(15 to 25 minutes)

Have someone read aloud 1 John 3:11-24 while people read along in their Bibles. Ask:

● **What does this passage tell us about God's desires for family relationships?** (We are to love each other; if we don't help each other we don't really love each other.)

● **What is the connection between God's love and our actions toward family members?** (If we really love God, we'll act lovingly toward family members; God's love should show through us.)

Say: **The first family God created was ripped apart by evil—Cain's murder of Abel. But God's love calls us to overcome fear and hate by loving with our actions as well as our words. Let's take a look at what else 1 John says about loving others.**

Form groups of four and have people read together 1 John 4:7-21. Have groups briefly discuss how this passage relates to our demonstrating love in family relationships. Then have groups brainstorm reasons family members don't get along and might fear or hate one another. Give groups about three or four minutes to list these on newsprint, then have them tape the newsprint to a wall.

After groups have completed their lists, have each group vote on the top two reasons from their list. Let everyone vote for two and tally which two get the most votes in each group. Have groups spend another three or four minutes brainstorming ways to live out love in response to those reasons.

For example, a group working with the reason "everyone in the family has different interests" might list love responses such as "spend time exploring one another's interests," "choose a night each week to learn about each other's interests," or "give family members space to explore their interests." Encourage people to come up with specific ideas for practical responses to the things that cause family distress.

Then have volunteers from each group tell the rest of the class the ideas they came up with for dealing with fear and hate in their families.

Say: **With God's love, we can confront and often defeat the fear and hate that can destroy families. But we must also learn to show love through our words and actions when we're *not* battling negative family situations. Even in the best of times, we can demonstrate God's love to family members.**

◀ THE POINT

■■■■■■■■■■■■■■■■■■■■■■■■■■

FOR *Even Deeper* DISCUSSION

Form groups of no more than four and discuss the following questions:

● According to 1 John 3:11-24, how do our actions toward our families reflect our status before God?

● In 1 John 3:16-17, we see a strong message about sharing material possessions. Do we take that message seriously enough? Explain.

● How does "the Spirit he gave us" help us know that Jesus lives in us (1 John 3:23-24)?

■■■■■■■■■■■■■■■■■■■■■■■■■■

APPLY▪IT▪TO **LIFE** THIS WEEK

The "Apply-It-To-Life This Week" handout (p. 36) helps people further explore the issues uncovered in today's class. Give everyone a photocopy of the handout. Encourage class members to take time during the coming week to explore the questions and activities listed on the handout.

CLOSING

Saying "I Love You"
(up to 10 minutes)

Form groups of three and assign each group one of the aspects of God's love (from the "God's Love" handout). Say: **In your group, come up with at least five specific ways you can show this aspect of God's love in your families through words or actions.**

Allow about three minutes for groups to brainstorm ideas. Then form three groups consisting of one person from each of the original smaller groups. Have people share what their small groups came up with.

Then have people list on their "God's Love" handouts specific things they'll do to demonstrate God's love to family members. Remind everyone that family members can include anyone from a spouse or a child to a parent or a grandparent or other relative. Encourage people to list family members' names next to the specific aspects of God's love they'll demonstrate to those people in the coming weeks.

When everyone is finished, say: **We've taken a good look today at how we can show God's love to others.** ▷ **As we go through this week,** ▷ **let's remember to demonstrate God's love to our family members.**

THE POINT ▷

For Extra Time

THE TOUGHEST PERSON TO LOVE
(up to 10 minutes)

Form pairs and have people tell their partners about the people in their families they find most difficult to love. Encourage honest discussion about this sensitive issue and remind people to help each other find ways to express God's love to these family members. Encourage partners to pray for God's help in showing love to each individual throughout the coming weeks.

LOVE CHECKLIST
(up to 10 minutes)

Give each person a sheet of paper (red paper if available) and a pencil. Have people tear full-sheet-sized heart shapes out of their papers. Have everyone work with partners to come up with six or more steps that will remind them to show God's love to family members at all times. For example, someone might include "Listen to the whole story before responding to a situation" and "Look for ways to develop trust in family members." Have people write their ideas on their heart shapes and commit to keeping them in a visible place at home as a "love reminder."

God's Love

In 1 Corinthians 13, Paul describes God's love. Next to at least three of the aspects of God's love listed below, write one sentence describing your experience of that aspect in relation to your family. You may describe how you live out (or don't live out) that aspect or how others in your family live out (or don't live out) that aspect. You'll be sharing these insights with your partner.

Aspects of God's Love

Patient

Kind

Not envious

Serving

Humble

Selfless

Slow to anger

Forgiving

Rejoicing in truth

Protecting

Trusting

Hopeful

Persevering

Winning

Discussion Questions

- Which aspect of God's love is most difficult to live out in your family? Explain.

- Which aspect of God's love is most needed in your family? Explain.

Permission to photocopy this handout from Group's Apply-It-To-Life™ Adult Bible Curriculum granted for local church use. Copyright © Group Publishing, Inc., Box 481, Loveland, CO 80539.

LESSON 2

I Love You

APPLY·IT·TO LIFE THIS WEEK

The Point: ▶ We can demonstrate God's love to family members.
Scripture Focus: 1 Corinthians 13:4-8; 1 John 3:11-24; and 1 John 4:7-21

Reflecting on God's Word

Each day this week, read one of the following passages and examine how the love you have for your family compares with the biblical love reflected in the Scripture. Then apply that message to what you believe about yourself. List your discoveries in the spaces under the passages.

Day 1: Deuteronomy 6:5. Love God with every part of us.

Day 2: Ephesians 3:17-19. Understand the depth of Christ's love.

Day 3: Galatians 5:6. Faith expresses itself through love.

Day 4: Jude 21. Remain in God's love.

Day 5: 1 John 3:16. Jesus demonstrated true love for us.

Day 6: Deuteronomy 10:12. Fear and serve God.

Beyond Reflection

1. Read Romans 5:8. How do you experience God's sacrificial love in your daily experience? In what family situations do you need to express a similar kind of love to family members?

2. Brainstorm a different way to say "I love you" to each member of your family for each day of the coming week. For example, you might write notes to family members one day, leave a message on the answering machine the next day, and buy a small gift as a token of your love on another day. Choose different options for each day, but always be sincere with your message.

3. Choose the person in your family who's most difficult to love and tell that person about your feelings. Be sensitive to the person's own feelings, but be honest about your difficulty in showing love to him or her. Then spend time in prayer (together if possible) asking God to help you demonstrate God's love more fully in your relationship.

Next Week's Bible Passages: Matthew 6:12-15; 18:21-35; and Colossians 3:12-14

Permission to photocopy this handout from Group's Apply-It-To-Life™ Adult Bible Curriculum granted for local church use.
Copyright © Group Publishing, Inc., Box 481, Loveland, CO 80539.

Lesson 3
I Forgive You

God wants us to forgive our family members as Christ has forgiven us.

◀ **THE POINT**

OBJECTIVES

Participants will
- discover why they need to be forgiven and to forgive,
- explore what the Bible teaches about how and why they should forgive, and
- experience being forgiven by God and practice forgiving their family members.

BIBLE BASIS

Look up the Scriptures. Then read the following background paragraphs to see how the passages relate to people today.

In **Matthew 18:21-35,** Jesus teaches Peter why he must forgive people as often as they need it.

As long as people have to spend time together, there will be conflicts. This is true of families as well as churches. Fortunately, Jesus knew this and explained how to resolve conflict in the church (Matthew 18:15-20). The offended party must take the initiative and do whatever is necessary to restore peace and harmony.

Peter saw a potential problem with Jesus' teaching. Jesus didn't limit the number of times someone would have to seek to repair a relationship damaged by sin. So Peter suggested a seven-sin limit on forgiveness. Since Jewish tradition required a person to forgive another only three times, Peter's offer seemed generous. But Jesus demanded even more. Peter (and every other Christian) should forgive the same person 77 times, that is, as often as forgiveness is needed (see Luke 17:4).

In the parable of the unmerciful servant (Matthew 18:23-34), Jesus explained why he could require such gen-

MATTHEW 18:21-35

erous forgiveness. In this parable, a king responded to a servant's plea for mercy and canceled that servant's huge debt. However, when that same servant imprisoned another servant who owed him a little money, the king became furious. He threw the first servant into jail and had him tortured.

Matthew 18:35 states the parable's point: God will not forgive us unless we forgive others. God can require us to forgive because our sins against him are vastly greater than the sins of others against us. (In the parable, the 10,000 talents was 600,000 times greater than the 100 denarii!) So when we accept forgiveness, we're obligated to forgive. When we refuse to forgive others, we're being disobedient to the one who has forgiven us for so much!

COLOSSIANS 3:12-14

In **Colossians 3:12-14,** Paul told the Christians at Colossae to forgive one another.

This passage gives a clear and direct command that we forgive others as Christ has forgiven us. Forgiveness isn't optional. Rather, forgiveness is an essential ingredient in healthy church (and family) relationships.

As God's special people, we are to develop virtues such as compassion, kindness, humility, gentleness, and patience in our lives. But regardless of how Christlike we become, we'll probably still offend and hurt others. That's why Paul told the Colossians to be patient with others as they grow and to forgive others when they fail. In short, God wants us to treat one another as Christ has treated us.

Forgiveness is a practical expression of the love that knits all of the virtues together. As Paul states elsewhere, love "keeps no record of wrongs" (1 Corinthians 13:5b). If we appreciate Christ's love for us, we'll extend love to others by erasing any record of their sins against us.

MATTHEW 6:12-15

In **Matthew 6:12-15,** Jesus teaches that only those who forgive will be forgiven.

Jesus used the Lord's Prayer (Matthew 6:9b-13) to teach his disciples how to pray. They were to praise God and ask for a variety of things, including God's working in the world, food for their daily needs, forgiveness, and safety from temptation. In the process, Jesus also taught his disciples (and us) some fundamental theological truths.

In verse 12, for example, Jesus implies that God will forgive us just as we have forgiven those who have sinned against us. It seems that Jesus is saying we must forgive others to be forgiven by God (see Luke 11:4). However, Jesus may also mean that God forgives us *in the same way* that we forgive others. If so, Jesus could be offering a variation of the Golden Rule (see Matthew 7:12); namely, that

God will do unto us as we do unto others. In any case, verses 14-15 state that God will forgive our sins only if we forgive others of their sins.

These biblical teachings on forgiveness can transform families. No family is perfect, and unfortunately, many are terribly imperfect. Jesus and Paul taught that forgiveness must play a key role in our family relationships. It may seem easier at times to forgive strangers, friends, or even enemies than to forgive family members who have hurt us. But since God has forgiven us of a debt of sin far beyond our ability to repay, we must forgive others, including our family members.

This Lesson at a Glance

Section	Minutes	What Participants Will Do	Supplies
Opening	up to 15	**Heavy Burdens**—Discover how the need to forgive and to be forgiven weighs us down.	Books
Bible Exploration and Application	20 to 30	☐ *Option 1:* **Hard to Forgive**—Identify who is difficult to forgive, discover from Matthew 18:21-35 why they should forgive, and commit to forgiving family members.	Bibles, "As Christ Forgives" handouts (p. 47), pencils
	15 to 20	☐ *Option 2:* **Letting Go**—Discover from Matthew 6:12-15 and Colossians 3:12-14 why they should forgive, then tear up cards symbolizing their need to be forgiven and to forgive.	Bibles, newsprint, marker, 3×5 cards, pencils, trash can
Closing	up to 10	**The Lord's Prayer**—Stress forgiveness while praying the Lord's Prayer.	Bibles
For Extra Time	up to 10	**I Have Been Forgiven**—Talk about times family members have forgiven them.	
	up to 10	**Global Forgiveness**—Discuss why some people and actions are harder to forgive than others.	Newspapers

OPENING

Heavy Burdens
(up to 15 minutes)

Before class, place a large supply of books (between five and 10 books for each person) on a table in the room. Church hymnals work well for this activity.

To begin class, invite people who attended last week to tell about the practical ways they expressed their love to family members in the previous week. Ask how their family members reacted to their expressions of love.

Then say: **Today we're going to focus on a key ingredient for developing a healthy family: forgiveness. We're going to explore how and why ▷ God wants us to forgive our family members as Christ has forgiven us.**

Have adults stand around the table with the books. If you have more than 10 people in your class, form groups of 10 or fewer and give each group access to a pile of books.

Read the following sentences one at a time, allowing time for everyone to perform the actions described. Class members should collect new books for each situation described until they're holding many books.

- **Pick up and hold one book for each family member who's hurt you through words or actions.**
- **Pick up and hold one book for each family member you've hurt through words or actions.**
- **Pick up and hold one book for each family member who's lied to you.**
- **Pick up and hold one book for each member of your family you've lied to.**
- **Pick up and hold one book for each family member who's been disrespectful toward you.**
- **Pick up and hold one book for each family member you've been disrespectful toward.**
- **Pick up and hold one book for each member of your family who's betrayed your trust.**
- **Pick up and hold one book for each member of your family whose trust you've betrayed.**

Tell class members to continue holding their books and to form groups of four. Some people may be carrying a lot of books, while others have few. Tell group members to hold the books in their laps while they discuss the following questions. After each question, have volunteers share their groups' responses with the rest of the class. Ask:

- **What does this activity tell us about our need for forgiveness in the family?** (We have lots of things to be forgiven for; family members hurt each other in a number of ways and need to ask for forgiveness.)

THE POINT ▷

TEACHER
TIP

If you don't have enough books for everyone in your class to do this activity individually, form pairs or small groups and have group members work together. If you use small groups, instruct group members to take turns holding and adding to the pile of books.

action words. Have each group discuss how their verb would work itself out in accepting other family members.

After another two minutes, have volunteers share how their words relate to accepting other family members.

Say: **When we act the way we've described in this activity, we learn to▶ accept and respect our family members. But talking about acceptance and doing it are often two different things. Think of one way to better accept a family member in the coming week and plan to do that thing this week.**

◀ THE POINT

After a moment or two of silence, have people form pairs (not with family members) and share with their partners their action plans for better accepting family members this week.

Then say: **Let's close today by making a commitment to accept family members no matter what the current status of their relationship with us.**

■■■■■■■■■■■■■■■■■■■■■■■■■■■■

FOR *Even Deeper* DISCUSSION

Form groups of no more than four and discuss the following questions:

● What makes it hardest to accept a family member? Why?

● Read Luke 18:29-30. How does what Jesus said in this passage relate to accepting family members? What was Jesus saying here?

● Can we be too accepting of family members who reject us or take advantage of us? Explain.

■■■■■■■■■■■■■■■■■■■■■■■■■■■■

APPLY·IT·TO **LIFE** THIS WEEK

The "Apply-It-To-Life This Week" handout (p. 26) helps people further explore the issues uncovered in today's class. Give everyone a photocopy of the handout. Encourage class members to take time during the coming week to explore the questions and activities listed on the handout.

CLOSING

Accept, Serve, and Honor
(up to 10 minutes)

THE POINT ▷

Say: **Think right now about one family member who might appreciate hearing a message of acceptance from you.**

Give each individual a sheet of paper and a pen or pencil. Have each person write a specific, personal message to at least one family member, expressing acceptance and love.

After everyone has written their messages, encourage them to write more messages after class. Say: **Give your messages to your family members this week. And remember, as we grow in Christ, ▷ we can learn to accept and respect family members more and more.**

⏱ For Extra Time

TOUGH TO ACCEPT
(up to 10 minutes)

Have people list reasons it's tough to accept family members. Then form groups of no more than four and have group members discuss ways the reasons on the list they just made relate to their own family situations. Encourage participants to find at least three reasons to accept a family member for each reason it's difficult to accept him or her.

PRAYER TIME
(up to 10 minutes)

Form groups of no more than four and have people share concerns about family relationships then pray together about those relationships.

• **How is the burden of carrying these books like the burden we carry when we don't forgive or ask for forgiveness?** (We're weighed down by sins; they make our lives heavy; they restrict our ability to enjoy our families.)

Have class members place their piles of books on the floor in the center of their groups. Ask:

• **What's it like to be rid of these books?** (It feels good to lose that burden; it's a relief.)

• **How is this like the feeling we have when we forgive or are forgiven? How is it different?** (It's similar because we feel like a load has been removed; it's different because true forgiveness is much harder to do.)

Say: **Because we're imperfect people in a fallen world, we have many things to forgive and be forgiven for. But forgiveness is such a freeing experience that ▷ God wants us to forgive family members just as Christ has forgiven us.**

◁ THE POINT

BIBLE EXPLORATION AND APPLICATION

☐ **OPTION 1:**

Hard to Forgive

(20 to 30 minutes)

Before class, make one photocopy of the "As Christ Forgives" handout (p. 47) for each person.

Find an open area in your room where everyone can stand, or move to a room, such as an auditorium, with plenty of open space.

Say: **Forgiveness is rarely easy, but sometimes we find it's especially hard to forgive certain people or actions. Let's find out what's really difficult for us to forgive. I'm going to read a series of questions asking you to choose which of two people would be harder for you to forgive. If the first person would be harder to forgive, stand on the side of the room to my right. If the second person would be harder to forgive, stand on my left.**

Read the following questions one at a time, allowing time for everyone to move into position. Tell class members that they must choose one side of the room or the other. After each situation, have everyone talk briefly with at least one partner (on the same side of the room) about why he or she chose that side of the room. Ask volunteers to share their reasons with the whole class. Ask: **Would it be harder for you to forgive...**

• **a family member who lied to you or a co-worker who lied to you?**

- a family member who told lies about you or a co-worker who spread rumors about you?
- a friend who cursed you or a friend who cursed God?
- someone who hurt you or someone who hurt your child?
- a parent who humiliated you or an employer who humiliated you?
- a political leader who embezzled money or a religious leader who embezzled money?
- a parent who committed adultery or a son or daughter who committed adultery?
- a parent who committed adultery or a spouse who committed adultery?
- a friend who accidentally killed a loved one or a stranger who accidentally killed a loved one?
- a Christian who cheated you or a non-Christian who cheated you?

After you read all of the questions, have class members form foursomes and discuss the following questions in their groups. Ask for volunteers to share their groups' insights after each question. Ask:

- **Which of the people described would be the easiest for you to forgive? Why?** Answers will vary.
- **Which of the people described would be the hardest for you to forgive? Why?** Answers will vary.

Then say: **Although we know intellectually that forgiveness is an important aspect of our Christian faith, it's not always an easy thing to put into practice. And sometimes family members are the most difficult people to forgive. But the Bible teaches that▷ God wants us to forgive our family members as Christ has forgiven us. Let's explore why.**

Have each group read Matthew 18:21-35. Then instruct groups to discuss the following questions. Ask volunteers to share their groups' answers after each question. Ask:

- **What did Jesus mean when he told Peter to forgive someone 77 times?** (Jesus wants us to forgive others as often as they need it; we should set no limit on forgiveness.)
- **According to verses 26-27, what did the first servant do to be forgiven?** (He asked for forgiveness; he promised to pay back all that he owed.)
- **According to verses 32-34, what did the first servant have to do to remain forgiven?** (He had to forgive others; he had to offer the same forgiveness to others that he had been given.)
- **According to verse 35, how will God treat us when we refuse to forgive others?** (God will hold us

THE POINT ▷

BIBLE INSIGHT

The Greek word for "forgive" in Matthew 18:21, 35 is *aphiemi*, which means "to let go" or "to send away." This word is often used to describe the release of a prisoner or the cancellation of a debt. In this passage, it is used to teach us to free those who sin against us, canceling their debt of sin and guilt. When we forgive people, we set them free and give up any leverage derived from their sin.

responsible for our sin; God will be angry with us; God won't forgive us.)

● **According to Jesus' parable, what does it mean to forgive?** (To cancel a debt someone owes you; to show mercy to someone who has sinned against you; to pardon a wrong someone has done to you.)

Say: **Since God has forgiven us, we need to forgive others, including our family members. Let's take a moment and begin to do that.**

Give each person a copy of the "As Christ Forgives" handout and a pencil. Have everyone complete the handout individually. Tell participants they won't have to share their completed handouts with other class members.

After approximately five minutes, say: **Use your handout as a springboard for forgiveness in your family. Take it home and refer to it when relationships with family members become difficult. Then ask God to help you forgive the ones you love because ▷ God wants us to forgive our family members as Christ forgave us.**

◁ **THE POINT**

■■■■■■■■■■■■■■■■■■■■■■■■■■■
FOR *Even Deeper* DISCUSSION

Form groups of no more than four and discuss the following questions:

● Read Matthew 18:15-20. What is our responsibility to people who don't know they've sinned against us? Is it possible to forgive people fully without them knowing it?

● Since God punishes those who don't forgive others (Matthew 18:35), is eternal life based on works? Does God punish us and still forgive us?

● What must we do to be forgiven by God?
■■■■■■■■■■■■■■■■■■■■■■■■■■■

☐ **OPTION 2:**
Letting Go
(15 to 20 minutes)

Form groups of four and tell group members to number off from one to four in their groups. Then direct the ones, twos, threes, and fours to different parts of the room. Have the ones and twos look up Colossians 3:12-14 and the threes and fours look up Matthew 6:12-15.

Say: **In your groups, read your passages and discuss what they say about forgiveness. Focus especially on what your passages say about how and why we should forgive our family members. After about five minutes, you'll rejoin your original groups and share your insights with them.**

To help guide the discussions, write the following questions on newsprint and hang it where everyone can see and easily refer to it.
- Why should we forgive family members?
- What happens when we don't forgive family members?
- What attitudes will enable us to forgive as Christ forgives?
- What's the difference between forgiving others and tolerating inappropriate behavior?

After about five minutes, have class members re-form their original groups and allow each person one minute to share his or her insights with the group. Encourage volunteers to tell the rest of the class what they discovered.

Then say: **God knows that it's easier for us to forgive others when we have already been forgiven. So let's put that into practice.**

Give each person in the class a 3×5 card and a pencil. Have a volunteer read aloud 1 John 1:9. Say: **On your 3×5 card, list any sins you committed against family members in the past that still bother or haunt you. You won't be showing this to anyone. This is between you and God.** Allow time for writing. **Now if you want to be forgiven, pray a silent prayer asking God for forgiveness.**

Next, have class members turn over their cards and write the names of family members they need to forgive. Direct everyone to pray silently again, using a prayer similar to this one: "Dear God, give me the love and power to forgive these family members."

Then instruct class members to tear their cards into small pieces. Say: **As you tear up your card, remember that Jesus has torn up or broken the power of guilt and sin in our lives. Just as Christ has forgiven us, we can now forgive family members.**

Have everyone stand, line up, and ceremonially proceed to the front to toss the pieces into a trash can. You may want to suggest that each class member keep one small piece of the card as a reminder to talk with family members he or she needs to ask for forgiveness. They may throw away the paper when they've followed through on this action.

Say: **In Ephesians 4:26, Paul says that we should not let the sun go down while we're still angry. But how can we speak the truth in love and release our anger each day?**

Have class members quickly call out practical ways to make forgiveness a part of everyday life and to avoid the hurt and alienation that build when people fail to forgive.

They might suggest ideas such as the following.
- Pray with family members at the end of each day.
- Instead of denying or burying hurt feelings, speak honestly about them when they occur.
- Ask for forgiveness as soon as you realize you've hurt a family member.
- Develop realistic expectations of family members.

Say: ▶ **God wants us to forgive our family members as Christ has forgiven us. Let's make a commitment to using the suggestions we've come up with to help our families become the kind of forgiving people God desires us to be.**

◀ THE POINT

For *Even Deeper* Discussion

Form groups of no more than four and discuss the following questions:
- Should people forgive parents or spouses who abuse them? To what extent should people maintain ongoing relationships with those family members?
- Matthew 6:14-15 says that God forgives only those who forgive others. Does that mean that our being forgiven is conditional? What else might be conditions of forgiveness?
- Should we forgive those who won't forgive us? Why or why not? How can we forgive people who don't know or won't admit that they need to be forgiven?

APPLY•IT•TO **LIFE** THIS WEEK The "Apply-It-To-Life This Week" handout (p. 48) helps people further explore the issues uncovered in today's class. Give everyone a photocopy of the handout. Encourage class members to take time during the coming week to explore the questions and activities listed on the handout.

Closing

The Lord's Prayer
(up to 10 minutes)

Form a circle and have everyone read or recite aloud the Lord's Prayer (Matthew 6:9b-13), repeating the verse about forgiveness (verse 12) seven times to symbolize that Jesus taught us to forgive others more than once. Pause after each verse 12 for class members to think about specific situations for which they need to forgive family members.

THE POINT ▷

Then say: ▷ **God wants us to forgive family members as Christ has forgiven us. To rejoice in the power God gives us to forgive and be forgiven, let's go around the room and encourage one another in Christ.**

Have each person choose his or her own way to encourage other class members, such as shaking hands, giving a high five, offering a hug, speaking kind words, or simply giving a smile. Then close by encouraging class members to approach their families this week with a new attitude toward forgiveness.

For Extra Time

I HAVE BEEN FORGIVEN
(up to 10 minutes)

Form trios and have trio members tell about times other family members (parent, spouse, child) forgave them when they didn't expect to be forgiven. Have adults discuss what it felt like to be forgiven and how that's like what it feels like to be forgiven by Christ.

GLOBAL FORGIVENESS
(up to 10 minutes)

Have small groups recount (or supply a stack of recent newspapers and have small groups find) recent newspaper stories describing actions that people must be forgiven for, such as murder, theft, or domestic violence. Then have groups rank the stories in order of the difficulty of forgiving the people involved. Ask groups to explain why certain actions would be harder to forgive than others. Then discuss ways to overcome hesitancies to forgive certain people.

As Christ Forgives

Follow the instructions to complete this handout. Be as honest as you possibly can. No one else will see what you write.

1. In your family, what actions do you find the most difficult to forgive?

2. List the names of family members you need to forgive and a word or phrase symbolizing what you need to forgive each of them for.

Name   **Reason I need to forgive**

3. Now determine when and how you'll forgive each person on your list and write that plan below.

Name   **When and how I'll forgive this person**

4. Finally, write a prayer asking God to forgive you for past sins and to give you strength to ask others for forgiveness.

Permission to photocopy this handout from Group's Apply-It-To-Life™ Adult Bible Curriculum granted for local church use.
Copyright © Group Publishing, Inc., Box 481, Loveland, CO 80539.

LESSON 3

I Forgive You

The Point: ▶ God wants us to forgive our family members as Christ has forgiven us.

Scripture Focus: Matthew 6:12-15; 18:21-35; and Colossians 3:12-14

APPLY•IT•TO LIFE THIS WEEK

Reflecting on God's Word

Each day this week, read one of the following Scripture passages and examine what it says about forgiveness. Then examine how well you are applying the message of the passage in your life. You may want to list your discoveries in the spaces under the passages.

Day 1: Exodus 34:6-7. God forgives and punishes Israel for making a golden calf.

Day 2: Luke 15:11-32. We should forgive those whom God has forgiven.

Day 3: Psalm 103:2-5. God forgives all of our sins and restores us.

Day 4: Luke 17:3-4. We should confront and forgive those who sin against us.

Day 5: Ephesians 1:3-8. God forgives us in Christ and through his blood.

Day 6: Ephesians 4:32. We should forgive others as Christ has forgiven us.

Beyond Reflection

1. Think of something you've done that's hurt a friend or family member. Then come up with a creative way to ask forgiveness for that action. For example, if you've hurt someone's feelings with the words you spoke, record a spoken message asking for that person's forgiveness.

2. Each morning, remember one specific thing God has forgiven you for. Then read Lamentations 3:22-23 and thank God for merciful forgiveness in that area of your life.

3. If your family is damaged by hurtful actions and words that people don't want to forgive or be forgiven for, consider talking with a church pastor or counselor to determine ways to bring forgiveness into your family. Then pray for your family daily and ask others at church to pray for your family, too.

Next Week's Bible Passages: Psalm 139:13-14; 145:1-7; and Acts 15:22-33

Permission to photocopy this handout from Group's Apply-It-To-Life™ Adult Bible Curriculum granted for local church use.
Copyright © Group Publishing, Inc., Box 481, Loveland, CO 80539.

Lesson 4

I Appreciate You

We can express sincere appreciation and thanks to family members.

◀ THE POINT

OBJECTIVES

Participants will
- examine how our thankfulness to family members relates to our thankfulness to God,
- experience the difficulty of giving praise, and
- express appreciation to family members in practical ways.

BIBLE BASIS

Look up the Scriptures. Then read the background paragraphs to see how the passages relate to people today.

In **Psalms 145:1-7 and 139:13-14,** the psalmist praises God.

PSALM 145:1-7; 139:13-14

The Psalms overflow with words of appreciation and thankfulness. The Israelites used these psalms or songs in worship services at the temple to honor and give thanks to God.

In Psalm 145, David praises God. David expresses his praise for God's greatness, goodness, and righteousness. He also praises God for the wonderful things he has done.

Many Psalms had titles in Hebrew, and most English translations include those titles. The title for Psalm 145 is the only psalm title that includes the Hebrew word for praise, from which the name Psalms was derived. This psalm, like many others, is also alphabetical, with its verses beginning with consecutive letters of the Hebrew alphabet. Perhaps this psalm could be seen as the model psalm, one for which the whole collection of Psalms was named.

In Psalm 139:13-14, David praises God for having created him. The Hebrew people viewed the development of a child within its mother as a great mystery. In this passage,

David credits God with directing the whole process. Even though human sin has affected all of us, God created us as incredibly complex, wonderfully designed beings.

We must remember that no matter how evil or good a person may seem, God created that person. We are not to praise other people the way we praise God, but we can certainly build others up through praise for the good things they do and for the abilities God has given them. And because God created every person, as we encourage and build others up through words of praise and appreciation we bring more glory and praise to God!

ACTS 15:22-33

In **Acts 15:22-33** we read about early Christian prophets delivering an encouraging message to a group of Christians.

Some legalistic Jewish Christians had gone to Antioch and criticized the non-Jewish Christians there because they hadn't been circumcised and weren't fulfilling all the other requirements of the Jewish law. But Paul and Barnabas disagreed with the legalists, telling people in Antioch that fulfilling those requirements was unnecessary. The Christians at Antioch were confused and troubled.

Paul and Barnabas brought the issue before the church leaders in Jerusalem, who ruled that Christians didn't need to fulfill all the requirements of the Jewish law. But they did need to follow a few guidelines based on principles the leaders felt were even higher than Jewish law, such as not eating meat offered to idols. The leaders in Jerusalem then wrote a letter to the Christians in Antioch telling them that they didn't need to be circumcised but that they should follow the guidelines being sent to them (Acts 15:29).

The church leaders then chose Judas and Silas to accompany Paul and Barnabas in delivering the letter. It probably wasn't a coincidence that Judas and Silas were prophets. In the New Testament, a primary role of prophets was to build up and encourage others. For Judas and Silas, delivering this message and affirming the Christians in Antioch was part of their ministry. God apparently thought that building people up was pretty important, since he gave certain people special abilities for that purpose.

God wants us to express thankfulness and appreciation in our families. Do we take our families for granted? Do we fail to say "thank you" to family members? Words of appreciation can brighten dark days. A simple "I really appreciate what you did!" can wonderfully lighten our steps. But many family members rarely hear such words.

Appreciation for others is rooted in a grateful attitude—a thankful spirit toward God. As we develop an attitude of praise to God, we'll also develop a natural ability to be thankful to and for our family members.

This Lesson at a Glance

Section	Minutes	What Participants Will Do	Supplies
Opening	up to 5	**Appreciation Time**—Learn what today's lesson is about.	
Bible Exploration and Application	20 to 30	☐ *Option 1:* **Attitude of Gratitude**—Examine Psalm 145:1-7 and 139:13-14, explore how the psalmist thanked God, and write their own psalms of appreciation.	Bibles, newsprint, marker, "The Thankful Me" handouts (p. 58), pencils
	25 to 35	☐ *Option 2:* **I Appreciate You**—Express appreciation to class members, read about encouragement given in Acts 15:22-33, and write letters of appreciation to family members.	Bibles, paper, pencils or pens
Closing	up to 5	**Appreciation Prayer**—Pray together for family praises and concerns.	
For Extra Time	up to 5	**Course Reflection**—Evaluate the effectiveness of this course.	
	up to 10	**Proverbial Family**—Scan chapters of Proverbs and discuss nuggets of wisdom for families.	Bibles, pencils or pens, paper

OPENING

Appreciation Time
(up to 5 minutes)

As class members gather, have volunteers share how forgiveness played a part in their relationships with family members over the past week. As you begin your class with prayer, thank God for his actions in families in the past week. Then encourage class members to get involved in the discussions and activities during the study.

To introduce today's lesson, use the following statement or your own summary of the main point: **Welcome to the final week of our study on affirming the family. We've explored the importance of accepting and respecting family members, loving family members, and making forgiveness a regular part of our family relationships. But one aspect of healthy families that often gets ignored is appreciating others.** ▷**We can express sincere appreciation and thanks to family members.**

THE POINT ▷

Today we'll explore ways to show our appreciation as we discover ways the psalmist showed his appreciation to God. As we get started, let's all give three or four people a pat on the back and tell them how glad we are that they're here today.

BIBLE EXPLORATION AND APPLICATION

☐ OPTION 1: Attitude of Gratitude
(20 to 30 minutes)

Before class, make enough copies of the "Thankful Me" handout (p. 58) so that each person may have one.

Invite three or four "ham" types or drama lovers to come forward and read aloud in unison Psalm 145:1-7. Encourage your readers to read the passage with the sincerity and enthusiasm they believe the author might have had when writing the psalm.

Allow your readers to sit down, then ask them:

● **What was it like to express praise to God the way you just did?** (Great; it made me feel joyful; it made me think about who God is.)

Ask the rest of the class:

● **How did it make you feel hearing this Psalm read with such enthusiasm and feeling?** (I felt good; it felt worshipful; I wanted to stand up with them.)

Ask everyone:

- **How is praising God similar to praising other people?** (Both say good things about the object of praise; both build up the receiver of praise.)
- **How is hearing God praised similar to receiving praise yourself?** (Both make us feel good; I like both because I like being praised and I like hearing God praised.)

Say: **The Bible contains a lot of praise for God. Let's take another look at Psalm 145 and see what we can learn about affirming family members.**

Have people call out things from Psalm 145 that the psalmist appreciates about God and list these on newsprint.

Then form groups of no more than four and distribute a copy of the "Thankful Me" handout (p. 58) and a pencil to each person. Have groups discuss the questions in part one of the handout. After five or six minutes, call time and have volunteers share insights from their small-group discussions.

Say: **Now I'd like you to complete part two of your handouts, writing your own psalm. You don't have to be a poet to write a short psalm. It doesn't even have to rhyme. Just write a sentence or two, or even a few words. In five minutes I'll collect the handouts and shuffle them before reading your psalms aloud to the class.**

Allow three minutes for adults to complete their handouts individually. Then collect the handouts, shuffle them, and read them aloud (without identifying the people who wrote them).

Afterward, ask:

- **What did you notice about these psalms in comparison with Psalm 145 and Psalm 139:13-14?** Answers will vary.
- **What was easy or difficult about writing these psalms?** (I didn't feel comfortable saying positive things about myself; it was easy to write something that was short and simple.)
- **What's the relationship between appreciation toward God and appreciation of your family members?** (Our appreciation toward each other is directly related to how much we appreciate God; we can only learn to appreciate each other in light of what God has done for each of us.)

Say: **The psalmist's thankfulness is a powerful reminder of our need to praise and thank God. And the more we learn to thank God for all he's done in the world, the more we can learn ▷ to express sincere appreciation and thanks to our family members.**

◁ **THE POINT**

■■■■■■■■■■■■■■■■■■■■■■■■■■■

FOR *Even Deeper*
DISCUSSION

Form groups of no more than four and discuss the following questions:

● Read 1 Corinthians 10:31. What does it mean to do something "for the glory of God"?

● How can we bring glory to God through our relationships? How can showing appreciation to family members bring glory to God?

● When might expressing appreciation to a family member do the most good? When might it do the least good?

■■■■■■■■■■■■■■■■■■■■■■■■■■■

☐ **OPTION 2:**

I Appreciate You

(25 to 35 minutes)

Have adults stand and mingle with other class members. Say: **During the next five minutes tell as many people as possible something you appreciate about them. For each person, complete this sentence: "What I really appreciate about you is..." Be specific in your appreciation and focus on things you've observed during this course or through other interactions you've had with each other in the past.**

Join in the appreciation time, making sure everyone receives words of appreciation.

Then form groups of no more than four to discuss the following questions:

● **Was this exercise easy or difficult? Why?** (It was easy because I knew the people well; it was difficult because I didn't know what to say.)

● **What was it like to be appreciated by class members?** (I liked it; I felt uncomfortable.)

● **How is this experience like or unlike appreciating family members?** (We aren't as upfront about thanking family members in real life; we like to thank each other often at home.)

Say: **Expressing appreciation to someone is a good way to provide encouragement. The Bible says a lot about how we are to encourage and affirm each other. Let's take a look at a passage that describes the encouragement the early church leaders showed to a certain group of people.**

While people are still in their groups of four, have them read Acts 15:22-33. You may want to give them some of the background information from the Bible Basis at the begin-

BIBLE INSIGHT

The letter to the Christians in Antioch came from the Jerusalem church leaders, the final authority in the whole church at the time. The encouraging letter told the people they were doing fine in their faith, in spite of what legalistic Jewish Christians had said. Notice that Judas and Silas—the ones delivering the message—didn't just hand them the letter and run. They also encouraged and built up the Christians there.

ning of the lesson or from the Bible Insight here. Then ask the following questions for them to discuss in their groups.

- **How was the effect of the appreciation we expressed a few minutes ago similar to the effect of the message delivered in this passage? How was it different?** (Both encouraged people; both made people glad; the message in the Bible was from a letter while ours was in person.)

- **How do you think the people in Antioch were strengthened?** (They became more confident in their faith because of the encouragement; they realized they were doing OK.)

- **How do you think our family members are strengthened by our encouragement and thanks?** (They realize we appreciate what they do; they may feel better about their progress.)

Say: **Earlier we expressed our appreciation to one another in class. Now we're going to express our appreciation for our family members through letters, similar to what the church leaders in Jerusalem did for the people in Antioch.**

Give each person one blank sheet of paper for each member of his or her family and a pencil or pen. Say: **Write notes to your family members telling them how much you appreciate the unique people God created them to be. Or express appreciation for something specific they've done recently. Be sincere and specific in your notes. This is an important part of wrapping up this course, so we're going to take about 15 minutes to do this.**

Use this time to write your own notes to family members. Then, after about 15 minutes, call time and encourage class members to finish their notes later if they haven't already done so. Ask class members to deliver their notes of appreciation in creative ways during the coming week (such as hiding them in lunch boxes, mailing them, or setting them on pillows at night).

Say: **A healthy family grows stronger when ▷ we express sincere appreciation and thanks to family members. After this course is over, let's continue our expressions of appreciation to family members.**

TEACHER TIP
A nice added touch for the notes to family members would be to use stationery or blank greeting cards if you have them available or could purchase them for the class.

TEACHER TIP
Some class members may not have immediate family members. Invite them to write notes to people who've been like family to them. These could include distant relatives, church members, or other friends.

◁ THE POINT

FOR *Even Deeper* DISCUSSION

Form groups of no more than four and discuss the following questions:

- Read Romans 15:1-6. In what way do the insults we express to people fall on Christ? In what way might our expressions of thanks to other people go to Christ?

● How does expressing appreciation for family members promote unity within the family and within the church?

● Read Hebrews 3:12-13. What reasons does this passage give for encouraging one another? Who would most likely become hardened: the person not giving encouragement or the person not receiving it?

■ ■

APPLY▪IT▪TO LIFE THIS WEEK The "Apply-It-To-Life This Week" handout (p. 59) helps people further explore the issues uncovered in today's class. Give everyone a photocopy of the handout. Encourage class members to take time during the coming week to explore the questions and activities listed on the handout.

CLOSING

Appreciation Prayer
(up to 5 minutes)

Have participants choose partners and stand facing each other. For one minute, have class members share prayer concerns about their families. Then have them share joys or praises about their families for another minute.

Say: **It's good to tell others about how we appreciate our family members, but it's even more important to ▷ express sincere appreciation to them. Let's work on doing that this week.**

THE POINT ▷

Lead class members in a closing prayer by having partners complete the following sentences:

● **Dear God, I thank you for my partner because...**

● **God, I thank you for my family because...**

● **God, help me as I commit to regularly encouraging my family members by...**

Ask class members what they liked most about the course and what they'd like to see different about it. Please note their comments (along with your own) and send them to the Adult Curriculum Editor at Group Publishing, Box 481, Loveland, Colorado 80539. We want your feedback so we can make each course we publish better than the last. Thanks!

For Extra Time

COURSE REFLECTION
(up to 5 minutes)

Have adults reflect on the past four lessons. Have them take turns completing the following sentences:
- Something I learned in this course was...
- If I could tell friends about this course, I'd say...
- Something I'll do differently because of this course is...

PROVERBIAL FAMILY
(up to 10 minutes)

Form three groups and assign each group one of the following series of chapters from Proverbs: chapters 1–10, chapters 11–20, and chapters 21–31. Give each group a sheet of paper and a pen or pencil.

Say: **The book of Proverbs is filled with wisdom for families. In your group, divide up your assigned chapters and find wise sayings for parents, children, and spouses. Jot down references you find.**

Allow about five minutes for groups to search their chapters. Then have groups report what they've discovered. After their reports, ask:
- **Which bit of family wisdom is most valuable to you?**
- **What wise advice could your family benefit from most? Explain.**
- **What do these verses tell us about the importance of appreciating family members?**

The Thankful Me

1. In your group, discuss the questions below, relating them to our list of things the psalmist appreciates about God.
   - What causes the psalmist to be thankful in these ways?
   - How does thankfulness toward each other grow out of thankfulness toward God?
   - How does thankfulness toward each other bring praise to God?
   - Is it easier to be thankful toward God or toward family members? Explain.

2. Read Psalm 139:13-14. In these verses the psalmist expresses his praise and appreciation for how God made him. In the space below, write your own psalm expressing your appreciation to God for who you are. Thank God for the positive attributes of your personality as well as the talents and gifts God's given you. If you have time, add verses praising God for your family members.

Permission to photocopy this handout from Group's Apply-It-To-Life™ Adult Bible Curriculum granted for local church use. Copyright © Group Publishing, Inc., Box 481, Loveland, CO 80539.

LESSON 4

I Appreciate You

APPLY·IT·TO LIFE THIS WEEK

The Point: ▶ We can express sincere appreciation and thanks to family members.
Scripture Focus: Psalm 145:1-7; 139:13-14; and Acts 15:22-33

Reflecting on God's Word

Each day this week, read one of the following Scripture passages and find out what we are to appreciate about God. List your discoveries in the spaces under the passages.

Day 1: Psalm 135:3. Praising God for his goodness.

Day 2: Psalm 107:8-9. Thanking God for his love.

Day 3: Psalm 103:1-5. Thanking God for all he does for us.

Day 4: Psalm 90:1-2. Praising God for his eternal nature.

Day 5: Psalm 23. Thanking God for his provision.

Day 6: Psalm 37:23-24. Thanking God for his protection.

Beyond Reflection

1. Brainstorm ways to appreciate a different member of your family each week for the next month (add or subtract weeks depending on the number of people in your family). Choose unique ways to appreciate family members, such as sending a singing telegram, taking a family member out for coffee or ice cream, or playing a favorite song with an uplifting message for your family member.

2. Write an appreciation letter to yourself on the back of this handout. Thank God for the qualities he's created in you. Read Psalms 8 and 139 for ideas on what to write. Then update your letter once every few months.

3. If you keep a journal, list in it daily one thing you appreciate about God and your family members.

Permission to photocopy this handout from Group's Apply-It-To-Life™ Adult Bible Curriculum granted for local church use. Copyright © Group Publishing, Inc., Box 481, Loveland, CO 80539.

Fellowship and Outreach Specials

Use the following activities any time you want. You can use them as part of (or in place of) your regular class activities, or you can plan a special event based on one or more of the ideas.

Photographs

Have adults bring their families and some family photographs to a special meeting celebrating the family. During the meeting, have participants present and describe their favorite family photos. People can also bring family trees or other information on family histories.

During the meeting, have someone take photographs of the attendees and make copies to give to the families represented.

Memories

Take your class members out for coffee and have them form groups of no more than four. Have groups sit together and recall favorite family memories. Use the following questions to start discussions:

- **What is your favorite holiday memory?**
- **When in your childhood were you happiest?**
- **Describe a special time with a parent or guardian.**
- **Where did your family go on vacations? What do you remember about family vacations?**

Funny Stories

Have a churchwide contest to find the funniest family stories. Have people in your class coordinate the event and choose judges who will determine the funniest, strangest, and most embarrassing family stories. Then invite children, teenagers, and adults to submit funny family stories. Remind people to get permission from the people involved in the story (if applicable) before submitting the story.

Hold a potluck dinner to celebrate the family, and award silly prizes for the funniest stories. You might want to collect the stories in written form and publish them in a booklet after the event.

Family Fun

Invite families to come up with fun activities they'd like your church to sponsor. Have children, teenagers, and adults submit their best ideas to the church leadership. Then ask your church to sponsor events that encourage full-family participation. Such events might include intergenerational retreats, whole-family sports events, and family entertainment nights.

Letters

Encourage class members to write letters to their family members and relatives, expressing their love and acceptance of those people. To make this easier, provide paper, stamps, and pens during a regular class period and encourage people to spend some of that time writing to family members.

Ways to Say I Love You

Photocopy the "Ways to Say I Love You" handout (p. 63) and give copies to people in your church. Encourage families to use these ideas to make saying "I love you" a fun and exciting experience.

Family Gathering

Plan a picnic or potluck dinner well in advance and invite families to attend. Plan lots of fun family activities including playing table games or volleyball, putting puzzles together, singing, and sharing favorite family memories. Consider making this an annual event.

Have someone videotape the party, making a record of the event. Each year at the family-gathering party, play the previous year's videotape, telling the continuing story of your church's families. Collect these tapes and keep them in your church library so people can check them out when they're looking for a positive picture of the family.

Ways to Say I Love You

When you're looking for ways to express love in your family, try some of these ideas:

- Have a picnic inside when it's cold outside.
- Send flowers.
- Fix the car.
- Leave a note under the windshield wiper.
- Bring back a souvenir from a trip.
- Wash the car together.
- Go to a movie together.
- Make each other lunch.
- Walk the dog together.
- Go to a park together and feed the ducks.
- Cook a special meal.
- Work in the yard together.
- Change the oil in the car.
- Iron clothes without being asked.
- Play video games together.
- Take out the garbage.
- Exercise together.
- Rent a hot tub and relax together.
- Pick apples together.
- Go on a mystery trip.
- Meet for a sunrise breakfast.
- Play board games together.
- Send thank you cards to each other.
- Do the dishes together.
- Apologize.
- Listen.
- Make each other laugh.
- Read poetry together.
- Play in the snow.
- Give a back rub.
- Write a family love song.
- Draw pictures of family members.
- Create a family banner.
- Go camping.
- Massage each other's feet.
- Shell pecans together.
- Choose a pumpkin or a Christmas tree together.
- Start a new holiday tradition.
- Create a family holiday of your own.
- Make a family video.
- Pray together each day.
- Take fun pictures of each other.
- Say "I love you."

Permission to photocopy this handout from Group's Apply-It-To-Life™ Adult Bible Curriculum granted for local church use. Copyright © Group Publishing, Inc., Box 481, Loveland, CO 80539.

Apply It To Life™ Adult
BIBLE CURRICULUM
from Group®

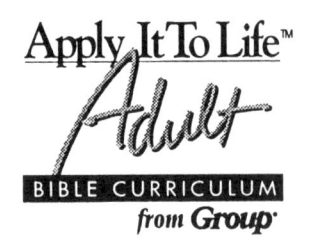

Now *One Book* Is All You'll Need to Get Any Size Adult Group Exploring...Discussing...Learning...and *Applying* God's Word!

Here's everything you need to lead any size class—in one money saving book!
- Complete 4-session courses!
- No extra student books needed!
- No waste—photocopiable handouts!
- Sure-fire discussion-starters included!

With **Apply-It-To-Life Adult Bible Curriculum**, you'll teach like Jesus taught—with *active learning*! Your adult learners will participate in activities and then share with others in the group. Together you'll grow in friendship...fellowship...and living out the Gospel.

Teach with confidence! Every lesson includes a thorough explanation of the Scripture text—you'll be prepared!

Teach new and mature Christians at the same time! You'll lead purposeful, nonthreatening discussions that let everyone participate...and learn!

Build relationships! Your adults want a close-knit group where they can feel at home. **Apply-It-To-Life** activities help your learners know and support one another as they apply Bible truths to their lives.

Get results! Each week's lesson is focused on *one* point that's thoroughly explored through every activity...discussion...application. Your adults will understand—and act on—what you teach.

TOPICS INCLUDE:

Title	ISBN
The Bible: What's in It for Me?	1-55945-504-7
The Church: What Am I Doing Here?	1-55945-513-6
Communication: Enhancing Your Relationships	1-55945-512-8
Evangelism for Every Day	1-55945-515-2
Faith in the Workplace	1-55945-514-4
Freedom: Seeing Yourself As God Sees You	1-55945-502-0
Jesus	1-55945-500-4
Strengthening Family Relationships	1-55945-501-2

...and many more!

Order today from your local Christian bookstore, or write: Group Publishing, Box 485, Loveland, CO 80539.